SOME NOTES
ON THE
PETRINE CLAIMS

SOME NOTES ON
THE PETRINE CLAIMS

BY
FRIEDRICH von HÜGEL

Friedrich
"freiherr von"
1852–1925

LONDON
SHEED & WARD
1930

FIRST PUBLISHED JUNE 1930
BY SHEED AND WARD
FROM 31 PATERNOSTER ROW
LONDON, E.C.4

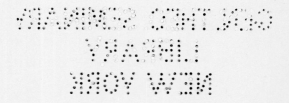

Printed in Great Britain by
Hazell Watson & Viney, Ltd., London and Aylesbury

PUBLISHERS' NOTE

THESE *Notes* were written by the late Baron Friedrich von Hügel for an intimate friend, who wishes to be anonymous. They are dated September 2–7, 1893, the *Post Scripta* September 17 of the same year.

No alteration of them has been made beyond the substitution of X for the High Anglican writer's name and the translation of French and German passages into English. The references given in the manuscript to these and to some English passages have been removed to an Appendix, to which the numerals given here in brackets after quotations refer.

CONTENTS

vii

CONTENTS

SOME NOTES ON THE PETRINE CLAIMS

My dear R,

I have been giving a careful study to X's two interesting letters, and as you ask me to answer —try to answer—them, I will now attempt to do so. But I will pass by the first, as it is but an exposition of the High Anglican position, without any proofs alleged. It is different with the second : it is a reasoned attack on the Roman position : I will try and meet it.

I have pencil-numbered his pages : it is to these numbers that my notes will refer.

I

ATTEMPT TO PRECISIONIZE THE POINT AT ISSUE

Now I should like first of all to make it a little clearer as to what exactly it is that we defend and that he attacks.

He says (pp. 2, 3) : " *The Roman Catholic answer is simplicity itself : the Holy Father as head of the Church on earth expresses the Church's mind, and his decisions are the All-Truth.*"

Is this correct ? It is of course true that we hold that that is *one* of the modes in which the Church has expressed, and does and will express, her mind ; but it is only one of several modes. General Councils have been held and been accepted as inerrant in their definitions by Roman Catholics before 1870 ; they will again be held and again so accepted after 1870. Again, it is the common teaching of our theologians, and indeed a necessary postulate of our position, that there is a third, the so-called passive infallibility, which secures that at no time could all the theologians and all the faithful of the Church unanimously and formally believe heresy and misunderstand the rulings of the actively infallible organs (Popes and Councils) in a formally heretical sense.

Is this so delightfully simple a scheme ? Whether true or untrue, it is *not* simple to the critical, philosophical and historical mind.

2

II

THE ALLEGED SUSPICIOUS SIMPLICITY OF POPERY

On p. 4 he says that *the very simplicity of the position makes him suspicious*. He adds very finely, and I agree with him *ex animo*, that *to believe what is right is on the same plane of difficulty as to do what is right* ; one involves just as long and tedious a strain as the other. He *suspects* such a short cut to Faith.

Now to this I shall make three counter-proposals :

(i) A religion meant for all the world must, if it be true, be capable of being put into as many forms of exposition as there are minds and classes to be won. If it cannot be put into a form capable of being " understood by the people " it might still be true as a closet science ; it could not claim to be the Faith destined to be apprehended by all mankind and to be saved by that apprehension and practical execution. But it must also, quite as really, be in its depth and breadth, in its genius and details capable of attracting and absorbing the subtlest and the deepest minds.

If we have our Neapolitan *lazzarone* and our

3

Irish beggar-woman, we have our Petau and our Newman, our Möhler and our Duchesne. Is there anything of the " short cut " temper about them ?

Take Petau, the French seventeenth-century Jesuit scholar. In his great *Dogmatic Theology* he had to treat of the history of the doctrine of the Holy Trinity, and, against the High Church Bishop Bull, shows how obscure, how incomplete, how halting, how positively incorrect is the language of many of the Fathers, pointing out how of the Tritheistic theory (heresy) " certain seeds may seem to have been cast in the old Fathers, not only in such as lived before Arius, but also in those who lived in the very midst of the Arian controversy " (*De Trinitate*, iv, 13).

A similar truly free and subtle attitude was taken up by Cardinal Newman, and is now represented by Abbé Duchesne.

Take Père Charles de Smedt, S. J., the Bollandist, writing on the organization of the early Church— a subject closely akin to X's—and see whether the following quotation gives a cruder view than that of the Branch Theory :

" I may be mistaken, but the study just undertaken seems to me to lead to the conclusion

4

that the Divine Founder of the Church did almost nothing personally, I mean by direct and obvious action, for its hierarchical organization. Apparently He remained within the organization of the Jewish synagogue. ' I have not come,' He said, ' to destroy the law, but to fulfil it.' The clearer revelation of supernatural truth which had been but obscurely hinted in the Old Testament ; the substitution of belief in the Messiah actually come for belief in the Messiah to come, also of the offering of the Eucharistic Victim for the bloody sacrifices of animals ; the institution of certain other mysterious rites ordained to place us in more intimate relations with the Godhead ; finally, the investiture of the Apostles with authority and commission to teach and to govern, with the grant to one of a primacy over the others—this, so far as I can see, constitutes the entire direct and obvious share of Jesus in the foundation of the Church.

" Men of genius, who undertake the foundation of a new and important institution which is to last and develop after their death, are careful to put together all the machinery with minute attention to detail, so that henceforward it may

in a sense function automatically in virtue of the
initial impetus and the perfect internal harmony
of its parts originally established, without anything being left to chance. At the very least
they entrust the continuation of their work to
particularly gifted disciples who have thoroughly
imbibed the spirit of their master and understood
his design, and are thus capable of realizing it
fully. Jesus, however, founding an institution
which according to His formal and express
promises was to endure to the end of time,
entrusted its government to the hands of unknown, rude, and uneducated men, grafted His
organization on that of a religious body imbued
with a narrow and exclusive nationalism, and
left to time and the manifold and diverse conditions of its environment the task of so modifying
this organization that it should correspond
perfectly with the needs of the new society
which was to spread throughout the entire world
and endure through all the ages. And the
transformation, effected unconsciously without
shocks or revolution, was a continuous progress
without a single retrograde step, until the
machinery had been built up, so complicated in
its details, so simple in its harmony, which we

6

admire to-day in the hierarchical constitution of the Catholic Church.

" What can be the explanation ? That Jesus, though vanishing from human eyes, always abides, living in the Church ; that by His supernatural providence He remains ever at the helm of His boat, to all appearance so frail and tossed by so many storms ; that His Spirit ever rests on those who occupy visibly His place among men and who, though for the most part unconscious of the fact, do nothing except under the impulse and guidance of this Divine Spirit. Indeed, the study of a development so wonderful should in my opinion suffice to extort from every man not blinded by invincible prejudices the cry of ardent admiration, *Digitus Dei est hic*." (1) And, with regard to the special point of this letter, he says :

" If I am not mistaken, the successors of St. Peter during the period with which we are concerned (the first three centuries) were, like the Prince of the Apostles himself, fully conscious of their prerogatives, and these were normally admitted in practice by the other bishops ; but they had not been clearly formulated as a theoretical principle incorporated into

7

the common teaching, and might therefore under special circumstances, in which they were opposed by obstinate prejudices or violently excited feelings, be temporarily obscured and insufficiently recognized." (2)

The fact is, I take it, that the human mind is so constituted that you cannot solve one difficulty without raising ten new ones, and that the Roman position both challenges rationalism and scepticism and stimulates thought and theological inquiry to a degree, or at least in a multiplicity of points and ways, far beyond Protestantism in all its forms, so fluid and so careful *not* to burn its ships behind it. We jut out like a rock into the ocean of the unknown ; they are like loam and rubble being eaten into by the sea : but this does not prevent the rock being dashed over and shaken by the waves. And, indeed, where do you find such a keen perception of the finiteness of all human thought and endeavour, of the incomprehensibleness of God (even in the world to come) and of all His mysteries, of the strange wonder of life, this fairy palace of our God, of the dark night of the soul and the piercing isolation of the secret heart, as in the great Catholic mystics, Papists pure and simple, such as St. Teresa and St. John of the Cross ?

(ii) " The proof of the pudding is in the eating." I entirely deny that, given an active, thoughtful mind, it is a determination to get a " short cut " that determines souls to come to us, or that our system necessarily produces such a temper of mind as that.

The trials of faith are *great* in the Roman Church : they are *different* from those of Protestantism, yes : but are they necessarily *less* ? Probably God only knows, and this no doubt varies with individual souls. But, ordinarily, souls will be tried in faith as well as conduct in proportion to the greatness of God's designs upon them. But for greatness of *trials*, as for greatness of graces and of ideals and of helps, commend me to the Roman Church.

St. Vincent de Paul, comforting himself for years with carrying about upon his person the Apostles' Creed in writing, as a sort of protest to God and to himself that he intended to believe and would sooner die than wilfully disbelieve in the dark night of that piercing desolation ; Cardinal Newman saying in print, at the end of thirty years of Rome, " I have had more to try me since I have been a Catholic than when I was an Anglican " ; perhaps, above all, what a devoted woman, who after being an admirable Anglican sister for twenty years became a Catholic and a Franciscan for another twenty, told a friend of mine who asked her what was the chief difference she had experienced during those two periods : " Only since I found the true Church, have I found the true Cross." These are some indications of what I mean. It is after all but an instance of that universal law of all life : the higher and fuller the life, the deeper the shadows as well as higher the lights, the more there is to sustain one and the more there is for one to bear.

(iii) And, finally, what is simple and consoling is not necessarily false. The angel who appeared to the shepherds on the night of the Nativity practically bade them take a short cut to the stable and the crib : they took it, and did wisely.

I take [it] that that simplicity is really suspicious, and always turns out to be false, which claims to leave no mystery, no perplexity, no room for patience and self-discipline. But only the most ignorant out- or insider could say this of the doctrine in question when properly understood and located in our system. I shall have occasion to illustrate this further on.

III

SUPPOSED PRESUMPTIONS AGAINST A VISIBLE HEAD

On pp. 4, 5 I find : " *It is taken for granted that the Church on earth must have a head on earth. Why? So far from being an obvious truth, to me it seems incredible. How can a body have two heads unless it is an abortion? . . . To argue for Christ as Head of the Church with a kind of a secondary changeable head for the Church on earth seems to my mind to insult our Blessed Lord, which is gross irreverence, and to argue the Church to be an abortion, which is illogical and unthinkable.* A priori *then, I see no reason to expect a head on earth : it is to me antecedently improbable : I start with a presumption against it, and if I am to be convinced that it is true I shall want overpowering argument to show it from the Bible and from the Apostolic and Patristic teaching.*"

Now these passages seem to me curiously instructive : they seem to show so clearly how there is nothing like the touchstone of Popery to bring out latent Protestantism. And by *Protestantism* I do not of course mean simply protest against the Pope ; I take the word in the High Church sense of the term.

For surely it is clear on reflection that the holders of a purely spiritual Church with but a spiritual Head, and again, Roman Catholics with their visible Church and a visible head, are both—whichever is right or wrong—consistent : an *a priori* objection to a visible head on the part of one who accepts a visible body is not.

If a visible body of pastors—each the head of his own parish, and of bishops—each the *absolute* head on earth (according to the High Church position) of his own diocese—if this is no " insult to our Blessed Lord," why should a visible head of the whole Church be such ? Each fragment —each diocese—according to X, is autonomous ; the more they are that, the more truly is the bishop the visible head of that part of the Church on earth : why is it not an insult to represent our Lord to ten thousand souls, whilst it *is* an insult to do so to two hundred million ?

The analogy of the body is scriptural : is it really far-fetched or unthinkable or insulting to think of an equally visible head, and after having comfortably accepted and thanked God for deacons, priests, bishops and patriarchs—I suppose Archbishop Benson considers himself that—as so many bonds and not bars between the spiritual soul and the Invisible God, to have no presumption, on the ground of illogicalness or insult, against the idea of one as much above the patriarchs as those are above the bishops, or as the bishops are above the priests ?

No, no ! In this matter there are, I think, but *two* consistent and indeed equally consistent presumptions : either Luther's, that *all* visible authority is a bar ; or the full Catholic one that *any* visible authority may be a bond. But all this of course is still in the region of presumptions.

IV

ACCEPTANCE OF THE VATICAN DEFINITION PERFECTLY REASONABLE FOR PAPISTS

Before going on the historical evidence, let me touch for one moment upon what I suppose is intended as a criticism on Papist logic. On p. 6, bottom, X. says of the " *thoroughgoing Papist* " and Papal Infallibility : " *It is enough for him* now *since the Vatican Council that it is a formulated dogma.*" I have not a word to say against this. But he goes on. " *The Pope says so, and he must know, so he is the head of the Church on earth and its infallible mouthpiece.*" We are involved in no such obvious vicious circle. Our position, admittedly since at least Photius's Schism, middle of ninth century, has been all along that the assembly of all the bishops in union with the Bishop of Rome form a General Council ; and that the solemn definitions of such Councils, if approved by the Pope, are infallible—this was quite as firmly held by a Gallican such as Bossuet as by an Ultramontane such as Fénelon—well, and such a General (Œcumenical) Council was that of the Vatican of 1870, and such a definition its definition of Papal Infallibility. There is not the shadow of a vicious circle here.

V

THE SCRIPTURE EVIDENCE : INTRODUCTORY

As to the Scripture evidence (pp. 7–10) I cannot quite make out whether X means to deny a strong or even any case for a primacy from the Gospels —a primacy not only of honour but one of jurisdiction—or only to deny that the middle and later chapters of the *Acts* and St. Paul's Epistles confirm or are indeed compatible with such an interpretation.

I can't quite make out, because though on p. 7 he says : " *We turn to the Bible : we read in the gospels of St. Peter : he is the foremost Apostle . . .*

St. Peter is the spokesman . . . St. Peter is the man of action," and further on : " *Turn to the Acts —the opening chapters strengthen our opinion of St. Peter's primacy. . . ,"* yet, on the other hand, after alluding to the council of Jerusalem and to St. Paul as the authoritative Teacher of Asia, Rome, etc., he concludes : " *And so the Bible record closes without giving to me at least any impression that St. Peter has any exceptional authority, or even any special influence more than others of the Apostles, except that which goes with his own private character.*"

I think it will be wisest to assume that he can hardly be very deeply impressed with the evidence of the Gospels for our Lord's having most solemnly promised him a quite exceptional authority ; for otherwise, our Lord being God, and His words of infinite depth and weight, He would bear with some obscurity, objections, and delay in their clear fulfilment, rather than in practice agree with —was it not Renan who called the " Thou art Peter " passage—" *ce malheureux calambour* " ?

I will take the scripture question under the three heads of Gospels ; Acts and Epistles ; St. Peter and St. John.

VI

THE GOSPELS : THE CRITICS' ADMISSIONS

Now I should like to make quite clear how, if we are determined to deny to St. Peter and his successors all legitimate claims to the primacy, we have not only to contradict a mass of later, and not much later, history ; but we have to hold that a most central, most crucial and impressive, most clear and precise, utterance of our Lord " has no ascertainable meaning " (so Whateley in his *Errors of Romanism*) ; or that it was intended to last but a lifetime, thirty years, and that our Lord either shared the Apostles' first idea that the end of the world would come then, or that He deliberately kept back the short duration of the privilege and as deliberately used words of the most impressive —surely over-impressive and misleading—import. (I understand that Mr. Gore holds to this solemnly promised primacy of thirty years or so : I should not wonder if, in, say, another thirty years, even the Neo-High-Church party may not have braced itself to think and even say the former of these two latter explanations.)

Now, to my mind, here indeed you would have an " insult to our Blessed Lord " : as God He

16

could and did foresee ; as God He could afford
to wait ; as our perfectioner and rewarder He
would wish to try our faith : I could then bear
with some obscurities, with some even great
difficulties ; but I could *not* bear to make His
most solemn words void, when I see them understood in their only natural and full meaning later
on in the Church, and believed in still and acted
upon by the largest body of Christians upon earth.

Now, that this is the *real* alternative, and not a
subjective bit of Popery, I think the following will
prove.

I am going to quote to you what Meyer, Weiss,
and Holtzmann say as to the Petrine texts in the
Gospels.   Let me explain who they are.

August Wilhelm Meyer (died 1873) devoted a
literary life of over forty years to New Testament
interpretation.   He was a Lutheran professor and
pastor, and his commentaries are admitted on all
hands as simply indispensable and as the great
standard books on the subject. Dr. Bernard
Weiss, also a Lutheran professor and pastor (still
alive, in Berlin), is the most learned of the now
living " orthodox " German Protestant commentators, and has re-edited the Commentaries of
Meyer on the Gospels and some of the Epistles.

Dr. Heinrich Holtzmann (still alive, in Strasburg) is a Lutheran professor of Scripture—the ablest of the living advanced-Left critics, who sniffs forgery and late ecclesiasticism wherever he can : he is so entirely " natural " in all his views that he cares not two straws as to what he says benefiting or damaging Rome or Wittenberg.

I am sure that no competent and candid student, whatever his theological views, would deny that each of these three, and still more these three together, represent best what is most worthy of consideration, and, where they agree, what is, in positive positions, most likely to be right, in latter nineteenth-century Protestant New Testament interpretation.

On *Matthew* xvi, 13–20, Meyer and Weiss say, after discussing our Lord's question to the Apostles :

Verses 16, *sqq.* As we should expect from his hasty temperament, and personal pre-eminence, also from the position promised him (*John* i, 43), Peter (the " mouth of the Apostles," as Chrysostom terms him) comes forward as spokesman, and decisively and solemnly declares Jesus the Messiah (the Christ) the Son of the living God (living in contrast with the dead gods of the heathen). These two together, the work and

18

nature of Jesus, constituted then and have constituted ever since the sum of the Christian creed.

Verse 17. " Simon Bar-Jona (son of Jona)." A solemn and formal mode of address . . . due to the importance of the declaration to follow. It is for his recognition of Jesus's Messiahship that Jesus pronounces Peter blessed, because it was only through a divine revelation that it could have been produced in him.

Verse 18. " But I say unto thee." It is for his utterance of a revelation from the Father, which singles him out from the rest, that Peter is declared blessed, and that now in return Jesus commends him and bestows upon him a lofty mission.

Πέτρος—an appellation : " Thou art a rock." The term ὁ πέτρος is current also in classical authors, and moreover not only with the less extensive signification, *stone*, as Homer always employs it in distinction from πέτρα, but also for *rock* (Plato, Sophocles, Pindar). The Gospels however have only the form πέτρα as a personal appellation, and the verbal discrepancy thus introduced was lacking only in the Aramaic original, in which the word used on both occasions was the same, *kepha*. Jesus declares Peter a

Rock for his firm and strong faith in Him, as affirmed in consequence of a particular revelation from God.

" And on this Rock." Here the emphasis lies on " *this*," ταύτῃ, by which Peter is pointed out—on no other rock than this ; that is to say, on this rock-nature, which like the rock in the parable (vii, 24 *sqq*.) is able to secure the stability of the house, the duration and unity of the new community which is to be founded.

" I will build my Church." I will build my community. That is to say, from the great *ecclesia* (the *qahal* of the Old Testament), the society of the Jewish people, those who believe in the Messiah will be picked out and formed into a special community, the community of Jesus Christ, which in accordance with a current metaphor (see the Epistles of St. Paul) is pictured as an edifice, of which Christ declares Himself the architect, and whose stability will be secured by Peter, the foundation on which it rests. The term *ecclesia*, however, was so consecrated by its theocratic associations that we need not, with Weisse, Bleek, and Holtzmann regard it as placed in the mouth of Jesus as the result of later conditions, especially in an utterance so

prophetic in character as this. Further, there
can be no doubt that a primacy among the
Apostles is here conferred upon Peter, inasmuch
as Christ selects him personally, as the man
whose apostolic activity shall—as the result of
his outstanding personality, grounded in his
firm faith—be the condition on which, from
the human point of view (*Apocalypse* xxi, 14 ;
Galatians ii, 9), is to depend the endurance and
stability of the society which Jesus will found
and foster. This is confirmed by his pre-
eminence in the *Acts*, and the actual position of
superiority which throughout the New Testament
we find this disciple occupying in the apostolic
circle (*Acts* xv, 7 ; ii, 14. *Galatians* i, 18 ;
ii, 7, 8). This primacy demands recognition
irrespective of confessional prejudices ; not so,
however, the deductions drawn from it by the
Roman Church. . . . The expedient to which
anti-Roman controversialists so frequently have
recourse, to explain the Rock as meaning not
Peter himself but his firm faith and its confession
(so Luther, Melancthon—also Calov, Ewald,
Zauge, Wiesehr, Keil) is inadmissible, since the
allusion to " this Rock," following as it does
the words " thou art a Rock " can refer only to

21

the Apostle himself, as also the succeeding words " I will give thee," though Peter's faith (more correctly the firm conviction which his confession displayed) was no doubt the reason why our Lord declared him the foundation-rock. This relationship (between his faith and mission) also underlies the application of Christ's words by the Fathers (Ambrose, Origen, Cyril, Chrysostom, Augustine) to the Apostle's faith.

Verse 19. " I will give." The future expresses a promise (no immediate grant), just as " I will build " refers to the future, when Christ will no longer command immediately and in person. The employment of the future tense is by itself sufficient proof that the office here in question is not that of preaching the gospel, the preaching which opens an entrance into the Kingdom of Heaven, as God prepares men's hearts. The metaphor of keys corresponds with the metaphorical " I will build " so far as the *ecclesia* (verse 18) in which the kingdom of heaven is immediately realized is pictured as a house whose doors are opened and shut by keys. In reference to Peter, however, the metaphor shifts, inasmuch as it changes from that of foundation-rock, not indeed to the inferior

22

metaphor of a porter but (*Luke* xii, 42 ;
I Corinthians iv, 1, 9, 17 ; *Titus* i, 7) to that of
the steward, expressing no longer the constant
relation of the Apostle to the Church but the
future authority which was its consequence. It
is the authority of the steward who is entrusted
with the supreme charge and supervision of the
economy of the household, and possesses full
powers of administration in it, symbolized by
the keys of the house (*Isaiah* xxii, 22 ; *Apocalypse*
iii, 7). To this authority belongs beyond all
doubt the right mentioned in these passages to
open and to shut.

" And whatsoever thou shalt bind" : a necessary appurtenance of this authority. And whatever thou shalt have forbidden on earth shall be
forbidden in heaven (by God), and what thou
shalt have permitted on earth shall be permitted
in heaven. (3)

Meyer explains the power of the keys as " the
authority to receive into or exclude from the future
Messianic kingdom ; in other words, to decide
whether a man shall enter it or not " ; and the
power of binding and loosing as follows : " It will
depend on thy decision, which will be held valid
before God, what shall be forbidden and exclude

the transgressor from the Messianic kingdom, and what shall be permitted and admit a man to that kingdom."

Weiss accepts neither of these interpretations. But it is impossible, I think, to make out more than his opinions as to what these two powers do *not* mean. (4)

Holtzmann on the same, *Matthew* xvi, 13–23 (for Holtzmann, as for most of the modern critics, St. Mark's gospel is, as a whole, older than St. Matthew's as a whole) :

The text common to *Matthew*, *Mark*, and *Luke* receives here an amplification pregnant with consequences of the utmost importance, namely the *Rock* passage peculiar to *Matthew* (xvii, 19). It takes the form of Jesus's counter-confession to that of Bar-jona, to whom not flesh and blood have given the knowledge of His Messiahship, and is fashioned on the pattern of the presentations of the *ecclesia* current in Jewish-Christian and Petrine circles. This term *ecclesia* represents in the Septuagint, as also in *Acts* vii, 38, *Hebrews* ii, 13, the Hebrew *qahal* and *esah*, and therefore signifies here the community of God, as it will be gathered together by the Messiah out of the old community founded

24

by Moses. But such an idea could only be reached after the body of the Messiah's disciples had emancipated itself from the framework of the old theocracy ; and therefore the designation in the mouth of Jesus . . . must be regarded as a Matthæan anticipation (so also Bleek). The message of Jesus referred to the Kingdom of Heaven ; the conception of the *ecclesia*, on the contrary, was introduced by Paul (and even he spoke of the *ecclesia Dei*, not yet of the *ecclesia Christi*) as also was the metaphor of a building (*I Corinthians* ; *Ephesians* ; *I Peter*).

Verse 18. The Pauline " pillar " (*Galatians* ii, 9) here becomes the foundation of the Church. For Jewish theology, as represented by *Isaiah* li, 1, 2, Abraham was regarded as the Rock on which God founded the world. Just such a Rock should Peter be for the Church. No doubt the usual meaning of πέτρος is *stone*, or *piece of rock*, but it was also employed with the sense of πέτρα, *rock*. In the Aramaic original in both places the word employed was *kepha* ; but in the Greek when the metaphor is applied to the person of Peter (and on this point the interpretation of Catholic exegetes must be accepted without qualification, in preference to the traditional Protestant exegesis, which explains the Rock as of Peter's faith or confession) on the first occasion the masculine form is necessarily used, though for this reason it is employed also as an appellation (*Mark* iii, 16). On the rock-nature thus manifested shall the Church abide, founded so firmly that the gates of the underworld (a metaphor taken from a palace, as in xii, 29) for all their strength (they never permit any one who has once entered to pass out again) shall not prevail against it.

The same man who just now was brought before us as the foundation of the building appears in verse 19 as the steward (see *Zacharias* xii, 42) and keybearer in the house when it has been built, like Jesus Himself in the house of His Father (*Apocalypse*, iii, 7). When Christ will no longer be present in person, Peter will exercise the supreme authority as steward and master of the house, symbolized by the keys which open and shut it (*Isaiah* xxii, 22).

The ecclesiastical spirit expressed throughout this entire *pericope* is specifically Catholic, as is shown by the identification of the concepts *Church* (verse 18) and *Kingdom of Heaven* (verse 19). The solemn proclamation of Peter's primacy, however, is in direct contradiction with *Mark* viii, 33, = *Matthew* xvi, 23, Jesus's most typical utterance about authority in His Kingdom (*Mark* ix, 35 ; x, 44) ; with the entire view of the apostolate presupposed by Paul, and the practical attitude which in consequence the Apostle of the Gentiles adopted to Peter. (5)

Meyer-Weiss on *Luke* xxii, 31–4 :

Verse 32. " But I " : spoken in consciousness of the superior power which as the result of His prayer He possessed to resist Satan's demand.

" For thee " : contrast the " you " above. " This entire utterance of our Lord presupposes that Peter is the first of the Apostles, whose firmness or fall determines the lesser or greater danger of the others." Bengel (Lutheran.)

" That thy faith fail not " : i.e. that thy faith in Me may not cease, that thou mayest not become unbelieving and fall away from Me. Jesus knew this prayer had been heard despite the temporary lapse of the denial, whose occurrence He equally foreknew. That is why He continues : " and thou (*thou*, the counterpart of *I*), once converted, confirm thy brethren (thy fellow-disciples ; be their support to uphold and strengthen them when their faith wavers)."

27

Meyer sees in this passage the office and duty of the primacy which will not be lost by a momentary fall. (6)

Meyer-Weiss on *John* xxi, 15, 23 :

Verse 15. " Feed my lambs." This cannot signify restoration to the apostolate, for the apostolic mission had been already bestowed upon him (Peter) together with all the others (xx, 21), and the apostolate is never spoken of as a pastoral office, that is to say, as an office of governing the community. Not only is the primacy in some sense or other included (Meyer, Luther, Godet, etc.), but the supreme government of the community (*Matthew* xvi, 18), cast away by his fall, is restored to him. *Cf.* Hengstenberg, and in the same sense Schanz, also Catholic exegetes. The arguments with which Keil, according to Steinmeyer, rejects restoration of any kind are altogether worthless. (7)

Holtzmann on this passage :

By the words " Feed my lambs," which contain a reference to x, 5, Peter is invested with the government of the community. Since, however, the apostolate has already been bestowed upon him in common with the other disciples (xx, 21–3), nothing but the supreme authority,

28

that is to say, his reinstatement in the position given him (*Matthew* xvi, 18, 19), can be intended here (Catholic exegetes, but also Hengstenberg, Weiss).

Verse 18. " Thou shalt stretch forth thy hands " refers to the carrying of the *furca* (so Wettstein), or rather the *patibulum* (the cross) which the *cruciarius* was compelled to drag on his neck with arms outstretched on it and pinioned to it. This, in contrast to the oriental method, was precisely the form of execution in use at Rome : *cf. II Peter* i, 14.

At a period when the Roman See already enjoyed a constantly increasing influence, which made itself felt in the Paschal controversy to which the Fourth Gospel alludes, and the day was no longer distant when Irenæus would catalogue an unbroken succession of bishops from Peter (III, iii, 3), it seemed no longer possible simply to pass over in silence the primacy of Peter in a work which sought to take up a definite position toward all contemporary powers. . . . Going still further in the direction taken in *Luke* xxii, 31–32, this appendix accordingly relates, in vv. 15, 17, Peter's reinstatement, his appointment not merely as an Apostle invested with the full apostolic commission, but actually as the Chief Shepherd of Christ's flock. (8)

VII

CONCLUSIONS FROM THESE ADMISSIONS

Now, before going on to *Acts* and *Galatians*, I should like to pause a little and draw some conclusions from the above facts and admissions—I, the half-foreign, whole-Papist : you can compare them with what has been or will be urged by the whole-English half-Catholics.

(i) First of all, please note the strength of the above combination : Meyer, Weiss, Holtzmann : and its practical conclusiveness when unanimous on a positive pro-Catholic point such as this. And notice further how, of the four contentions which make up the Catholic Petrine claims—(*a*) our Lord conferred a primacy of jurisdiction on St. Peter ; (*b*) St. Peter was in Rome and was martyred there ; (*c*) St. Peter was first Head of the Church of Rome (whether his title was " Bishop " or what not is immaterial) ; (*d*) the primacy and privilege of St. Peter was intended to descend to his successors—the first two are now fully conceded, or at least no more flatly denied by all the best Protestant and sceptical scholars of the day. With regard to the primacy, the above quotations must suffice. As to sojourn and martyrdom in Rome, it will be sufficient to remind you that such different non-Catholic scholars as the cautious, anti-sacerdotalist, first-class authority, Bishop Lightfoot (he held both proved) ; Ernest Renan ; Dr. Salmon, the Irish Protestant scholar in his Trinity College (Dublin) lectures to Irish Protestant undergraduates (both proved) ; Dr. Adolph Harnack, the first-rate, though intensely sceptical and deeply anti-dogmatic and anti-hierarchical Berlin authority —at least as to the sojourn : " that Peter was in Rome is in the highest degree probable " (9) ; and finally Holtzmann in the quotation [on page 29] (at least as regards the writer of *John* xxi, 18 believing, or intending his readers to believe, that St. Peter was in Rome and was martyred there)—all agree in positively affirming or at least in inclining to affirm at least the sojourn, and most of them the martyrdom, in Rome.

And notice finally, that it has taken our Protestant friends three centuries to generally come to admit half of the Catholic points which they scouted with an energy even greater than they still repudiate the other half : and that one has to have some learning to be fully aware of the change, so generally are they silent as to their past attitude, and so sure do they appear in such arguments as they still urge against Rome.

(ii) Again, take note how the Gospels contain no serious difficulty whatsoever against the primacy of St. Peter. For what Holtzmann quotes—the only two passages he can find (above p. 27)—really deserve no serious consideration. *Mark* viii, 33 =*Matthew* xvi, 23—the " Get behind me, Satan," spoken by our Lord to Peter after His promise to him of the primacy in the future—is easily met, if we remember first, that it was the Potter addressing His own clay, and that our Lord was far more above St. Peter than any one could be below St. Peter ; and secondly, that it was spoken between the promise and its fulfilment, and not (if that had been possible) afterwards : even one of the other Apostles could have rebuked St. Peter during that period without raising any serious difficulty against the primacy, which in its fulness was only to date from the Ascension. And *Mark* ix, 35, 44, means surely no more than what Meyer and Weiss make it mean : " Only in service and self-denial should one try to surpass another." (10)

As well could you use St. John of the Cross's burning denunciations of love of high ecclesiastical position as an " abomination before God " as a proof that he denied the legitimacy of bishops and the Pope.

(iii) I quite admit that parts of *Acts* and of St. Paul's Epistles *are* difficulties. But before proceeding to them, let me draw your attention to the following, which (no doubt through my insufficient reading of recent books on the subject) I have nowhere seen even alluded to, but which seems to me unanswerable to anyone who is fully penetrated by the fact (with the critics I have mentioned) that *Matthew*, *Luke*, *John do* teach the Petrine primacy and nothing short of it.

The point I am thinking of is the following :

As you know, our Lord's Crucifixion is best dated as in the year A.D. 30, the Council of Jerusalem as in the year 50 or 51 ; the composition of the *Epistle to the Galatians* as in the year 57 or 58. Now, the Gospels that concern us date—the Aramaic *St. Matthew* probably between 65 and 70, our present *St. Matthew* soon after 70 ; *St. Luke*, probably soon after 70, though some of the sceptics bring him down (very unreasonably) as

D   33

low as 100–120 ; *St. John*, if written, as we have the book, by the Apostle, between 90 and 100 ; if developed by disciples of his, between 100 and 110. Anyhow, what is quite certain is that the Council and the composition of *Galatians* lay behind the writer of our present *St. Matthew* by at least twenty and fourteen years respectively ; lay behind St. Luke when writing his Gospel by at least the same time ; lay behind the author of the Fourth Gospel by forty to sixty and about thirty to fifty years respectively.

Again, as to dependence and school and residence of the authors, it is certain that neither of the three were immediate disciples of St. Peter, though St. Matthew belongs to his school. But St. Luke is an immediate disciple of St. Paul, and overflowing with special knowledge of St. Paul and special unison with his spirit. And the author of the Fourth Gospel is either the Beloved Disciple himself or at the very least an immediate disciple of his, editing his master's memoirs. " St. Matthew " very probably wrote in Palestine—the Aramaic Matthew the Apostle all but certainly ; St. Luke very probably in Rome ; St. John certainly in Ephesus.

Now, pray notice what follows from this. Here

we have three writers, of three distinct schools and only one of these schools that of St. Peter ; they all three write after, and one of them half a century or nearly after, both the institution and restoration of the primacy on the one hand, and the events recorded in *Acts* and *Galatians* (that are supposed to be fatal against it) on the other hand ; one of these writers is full of the innermost mind of St. Paul ; the other has reclined on our Lord's breast and drunk deepest of His spirit—and they all three are so little aware of the incompatibility of these two sets of events that they give the first set with a precision and solemnity and prominence which, if the second set of events and, allow me to say, above all, if Popery were not in existence, would be accepted by all as bearing but one possible meaning.

Now, what are we to gather from this ? I can find but one answer. That the contradiction between the two sets of facts is but apparent, or at least not fundamental : that neither St. Luke nor St. John, nor indeed St. Matthew for the matter of that, could have written in the manner they have done if they had held the Protestant (even the High Church) view and had interpreted St. Paul's words and actions as anti-Romans

interpret them—we have a set of facts and a set
of narrations concerning these facts, two of the
narrators (St. Matthew, the author of the Aramaic
Gospel, and St. John) actually spectators, indeed
participants, in the scenes described, and the third
an immediate disciple of the very man who is
supposed to finally dispose of these facts—and
yet all three narratives press upon us the same
conclusion as to the first set of facts and against
the Protestant interpretation of the second set.
Can any of us know St. Paul's mind as well as
St. Luke did ? Or our Lord's own mind as well
as St. John ? Can we know the facts of the
Council and the meaning of the Epistle as well as
they both, as all three writers, did ?

(iv) Finally, note over how long a period, how
far back, we can take, and how low down we can
bring the evidence for the belief in the primacy
in Apostolic times.

All the best critics hold that though our present
St. Matthew is probably some five to ten years
less old than our *St. Mark*, yet that the Aramaic
St. Matthew (probably or at least possibly identical
with a collection of sayings of our Lord we know
to have been in existence before A.D. 70) was really

written by the Apostle, was the earliest written Gospel, is to be still found in the parts of our present *St. Matthew* which record our Lord's discourses and sayings, and that this *Proto-Matthew* already contained the " Thou art Peter."

Again, the Fourth Gospel is by the last of the New Testament writers, indeed, the last New Testament document, with the sole exception of the three *Epistles* of St. John : and the last chapter of this last of the bigger books of the New Testament contains a solemn reaffirmation of the primacy. This, sixty years after Cæsarea Philippi, forty and thirty years after the Council of Jerusalem and the *Epistle to the Galatians*, twenty-five years after St. Peter's death. And it is put as the final note of the Gospel, and in contrast to the Beloved Disciple's vocation and position—and is so put by that Disciple himself, or at the very least by one of his immediate *entourage*. And it is put, as Holtzmann well feels, not as of antiquarian interest, but as of living importance : Peter was gone, but a great principle remained.

And between the practical, Jewish-Christian, objective First Gospeller and the mystical, Platonist, subjective or rather reflective, theological Last Gospeller, comes the thoroughly Pauline heathen-

Christian writer of the Third Gospel ; and the sixties, the seventies and the nineties—Judæa, Rome, and Ephesus—all teach one lesson and bid us not explain away our Lord's promises for the sake of difficulties which they had before them in all their fulness.

VIII

ACTS AND EPISTLES

Now, as to *Acts* and Epistles. I will first take the Council and St. Peter's attitude in the *Acts* generally first. St. Paul's general overshadowing of St. Peter I will take together with the St. Peter and St. John point.

I am glad to see that X admits that *the opening chapters of the* Acts *confirm one's opinion of St. Peter's primacy* (p. 9) : I should, however, like to quote the following pregnant passage from Döllinger :

Among the apostles St. Peter asserts a pre-eminence which it never occurred to any of the others to contest. He has received the keys of the Kingdom, and is the rock on which the Church has been built ; that is to say, the stability, growth, and prosperity of the Church are based on the office established in his person.

It is his function to strengthen his brethren and pasture Christ's flock. To him, as Paul says, the Lord has entrusted in a very special manner the "gospel of the circumcision," as to the apostle from Tarsus the "gospel of the uncircumcision" (*Galatians* ii, 7). Christ Himself was "made a minister of the circumcision" (*Romans* xv, 8), His work as Messiah was directed to the flock of Israel, as He Himself said: "I am not sent but unto the lost sheep of the house of Israel" (*Matthew* xv, 24; *cf.* xx, 28). In this Peter was Jesus's successor. He is in a peculiar sense the Apostle of Israel, the Head of the Church of the Circumcision, and this in a higher and more privileged fashion than James, whose status was inferior in two respects: first, because his authority was restricted to Jerusalem, whereas Peter from the outset embraced the entire Diaspora in the field of his mission; secondly, because he always kept apart from the Gentiles, whereas it was Peter who first admitted them into the Church, and moreover the scope of his mission extended, though subordinately, to the converted Gentiles. For there were not two churches, a church of the circumcised, and another church of the uncircumcised, but one

only olive tree, one people of God, one Israel
(*Romans* xi, 24), and into this tree the Gentiles
were grafted, thereby, as adopted children of
Abraham, being made partakers of the root and
sap of the olive. Hence it is that Peter tells the
believing women of the communities to whom
his epistle is addressed that they have become
" Sarah's daughters " (1 *Peter* iii, 6), for another
passage (iv, 3, 4) shows that the letter is addressed
to communities composed predominantly of
Gentiles. Therefore the Apostle to whose charge
Israel has been specially committed by God is
necessarily the head of the apostolic college and
the entire Church. The arrangement concluded
between Paul and himself effected a division of
labour, not a division of the Church ; and
Paul, whose special object in visiting Jerusalem
was to spend fifteen days with Peter, was well
aware that of the three " pillar " Apostles Cephas
was the chief, though at the same time he would
not allow that his execution of the mission
bestowed upon him by divine call and revelation
depended on Peter, and actually opposed him
at Antioch. The issue to which Paul attached
such fundamental importance—whether the Gentiles should be converted to Christ directly or

as proselytes to Judaism—had been first decided
not by himself but by Peter, in consequence of
a special revelation. Nor was it until after that
fifteen days' visit to Peter that Paul entered upon
his peculiar office, the apostolate of the Gentiles.

So long as the Apostles remained together in
Jerusalem, Peter's primacy was manifested on
every occasion of importance. He it was who
arranged for the completion of the apostolic
college by the election of Matthias. He decided
the form of the election, and restricted the
choice to those who had been constant com-
panions of Christ and witnesses of His teaching
and deeds. He was the spokesman both before
the people and the Sanhedrim, and worked the
first miracle to prove the Resurrection of Christ.
The condemnation pronounced on Ananias and
Sapphira, the anathema launched against Simon,
the first heretic, the first visitation and strengthen-
ing of the churches oppressed by persecution—
all these were his work. And if he was sent together with John by the apostolic college to the
new converts in Samaria, he was himself a member of that college and, indeed, its president.
After the same fashion the Jews sent their high
priest Ismael to Nero (Josephus, *Ant. Jud.*, xx,

7), and Ignatius tells us that the neighbouring churches in Asia had sent, some their bishops, others their presbyters or deacons (*Philad*., 10). As everywhere and always, Peter occupied the chief position at the Council of Jerusalem, which declared the Gentiles free from the obligation to observe the ritual Law. He opened the Council, and his opinion, together with the amendments suggested by James, was accepted as the official decision.

At this Council James's judgment must have carried particular weight, as Peter was to a certain extent a party to the dispute, as well as Paul. It was known in Jerusalem that at Cæsarea he had ordered Cornelius the centurion and other Gentiles to be baptized without circumcision, a step which had already provoked strong opposition on his return to Jerusalem. And now when Paul and Barnabas had come up to Jerusalem and the Council was to be held, certain believing Pharisees again brought forward the demand that the Gentiles must accept circumcision and the Law (*Acts* xv, 5). Under these circumstances James, who with his entire community observed the Law, was the most suitable judge to convince the opposition in this dispute, and it is obvious why the decree was drawn up in conformity with his opinion. It was for the same reason that Paul, when in the *Epistle to the Galatians* he appeals to the " pillar " Apostles, who had extended to him and Barnabas the right hand of fellowship, mentions James first and before Kephas (*Galatians* ii, 9). For in the actual situation, and for opponents who no doubt invoked the precedent of the mother-church, which observed the Law, the example of James was of greater weight than Peter's, as later on the Ebionites were at pains to claim for themselves the authority of James as the highest in the Church. But James himself recognized that it was Peter who had received the divine commission to gather from the Gentiles a people to bear God's name and to unite them together with the believing Jews in one Church (*Acts* xv, 14). For he subscribes Peter's claim that God had chosen him of all men to preach to the Gentiles. That charge befitted the Apostle who alone had received the keys of the Kingdom. Therefore Paul entered later upon the work begun by Peter, and built on the foundation he had laid. This he could not have done, had not Peter as a result of their earlier agreement recognized him as a divinely called fellow-worker, although Paul derived his actual commission immediately from Christ.

That Paul's position was inferior to Peter's is shown by the way in which he speaks of his relation to the Jews and Gentiles : he strives with all his might to glorify his office as Apostle of the Gentiles by numerous conversions, that (as a result of the converts thus made) he may provoke some of his own people to jealousy and so win them (*Romans* xi, 13, 14). Peter had no need of this indirect route. With all the weight attaching to his office he worked with powerful effect among Jews as well as Gentiles, and it was a self-imposed restriction which later made him choose the Jews rather than the Gentiles as the sphere of his labours.

Moreover, Paul himself made no attempt to conceal the fact that for him also Peter was not simply one of the Twelve, but possessed a unique position and dignity, distinct from all the rest, and therefore that the appeal to his example carried a special weight. He was not content to say " Have I not like the other Apostles the right to take a sister about with me ? " but he says " like the other Apostles, the brethren of

44

the Lord and Kephas " (*I Corinthians* ix, 5). [Notice, please, there are three ascending ranks, the lowest occupied by eleven, the middle by some three or four, perhaps, the top by one alone : Peter.]   And if on his part Peter in his exhortation to the presbyters of the churches called himself their " fellow presbyter," it was because he remembered the precept and example of the Lord, and acted as the follower of Him who, though His position was so high above theirs, had called the Apostles His " brethren " (*Matthew* xxviii, 10), and had bidden him strengthen his " brethren " (*Luke* xxii, 32), and as the greatest in the Kingdom to be at the same time the least and humblest.   He saw in the presbyters men who like himself served the brethren by their teaching and government, and were so far sharers of his office.   Thus, too, Peter, as the first of the Apostles, is the one who insists most emphatically that office in the Church is simply guidance, service, the setting a good example, but no lordship, and warns every member of the clergy against the lust of domination (*I Peter* v, 3). (11)

As to the conflict at Antioch, I will quote the following extract from a long discussion :

Now it was Peter who at the Council had himself declared the observance of the ritual Law a yoke which neither the believing Jews nor their fathers had been able to bear, and who moreover had, as Paul expressed it, " although a Jew lived after the fashion of a Gentile (*Galatians* ii, 14) and not after the fashion of a Jew." Now, however, he adopted an attitude which, in view of his position in the Church, amounted to a moral compulsion upon the Gentile converts to submit to the yoke of the Law. For if the organ of juridical unity, the man whom Christ had chosen to be the shepherd of His flock, proclaimed by his conduct that in his eyes the uncircumcised were unclean, their persons and food a source of defilement, the latter could only conclude that if they would be admitted to fellowship with the head of the Church the sole course open to them was to sacrifice the liberty granted them by the Council and also become observers of the Law. To Paul, from his standpoint as Apostle of the Gentiles and messenger of the Gospel-freedom, this was intolerable ; moreover, he considered the abuse which the party of Pharisaic zealots, who wished to have imposed on the Gentile

46

converts the yoke of the entire Law, would make of the example set by the Prince of the Apostles. Publicly and in sharp terms he denounced Peter's conduct. . . . [And then he gives St. Paul's words, *Galatians* ii, 11–18, and concludes :]

We are not told what reply Peter made. In any case the misunderstanding was not lasting, for on the main issue both Apostles were agreed. (12)

Which Döllinger proceeds to prove : indeed, I do not know anyone who would, unless he be a Tübingen *a priori* man, deny this.

Now, I think the above quotations are sufficient, if not fully to meet the difficulties raised by the specific statements of *Acts* and *Galatians*, at least to reduce them to such a compass as to be quite bearable by my argument under No. VII. Besides these specific statements, there remains the general question of the overshadowing influence in the Church of SS. Paul and John, and as I not only fully admit it with all the world, but look upon it as typical and of vital importance, I will treat of it in a moment.

I only pause for an instant to point out that if St. Paul's conflict with St. Peter is compatible with

the primacy and with the former's belief in it—
how careful we should be in our conclusions, I will
not say from the silence of saints, but even from
their apparently most unreserved conflicts with
the Roman See ! Years ago, I was urged by High
and Low Protestants to study the case of Savonarola
as an enlightening one : and, indeed, it would seem
a test case. Here is a man who, if not a saint,
was the admired of canonized saints (St. Philip
Neri and Catherine de Ricci), declared by Pope
Benedict XIV to be not unworthy of canonization,
a man of heroic mould. And he is pitted against
the worst of the popes ; appeals to a General
Council to depose him ; refuses to go to Rome
(here he was contumacious, I think) ; denounces
the Pope in unmeasured terms ; and dies excommunicate and in the flames at this worst Pope's
instigation and orders. And (at least the *whole*)
Protestants look upon him as a precursor of Luther,
and have actually put his statue amongst Luther's
precursors on to the Luther monument at Worms.
And yet for all and for all that : " *il n'en est rien.*"
It was Savonarola's very zeal and burning belief
in the Papacy and its divinely constituted rights
and duties, his very hunger and thirst for a *Pope*
Angelico, that made him break out, hero but not

saint that he was, into utterances, taken singly, not always unlike those of the later " Reformers " who as strongly hated the idea of the Papacy at its best as the worst faults and sins of its poorest representatives at their worst.

For one thing, please realize and remember that although the gradual development of the Petrine prerogatives has gradually led up to the two Vatican decrees, yet those very decrees make it (as always) abundantly clear that, whilst the Pope is both supreme Ruler and supreme Doctor in the Church, it is *only as supreme Doctor that he is*, or even claims to be, *inerrant*. Sixtus V excommunicated Elizabeth, and Pius IX excommunicated Victor Emmanuel : they may both have erred in so doing. Mediæval popes have again and again laid the interdict upon whole countries : all Catholic Church-historians of the first rank admit that at least several times it was done wrongly, or at least excessively, and saints have gone and ministered to the sick and dying notwithstanding the Papal action. Interior assent to the Pope's *ex cathedra* pronouncements is *always* due ; obedience to the Pope's governmental orders is *generally* and *presumptively* due. Saints have at times passively disobeyed single orders or have remon-

E   49

strated with the popes as to their neglect of duty or misleading and ambiguous attitude : in this latter sense St. Peter might have justly been called " heretical " by St. Paul, as Pope Honorius was condemned as " heretical " by the Sixth General Council. But clear cases of saints denying the primacy itself, or persisting in a state of excommunication without making efforts at reconciliation—such cases are at the very least so rare as to demand, in consistency, the kind of treatment scholarly Anglicans, and indeed all dogmatic and ecclesiastical Christians, give to the questions of the development of the institution of the episcopate and of the doctrine of the Holy Trinity—of which more under No. X.

IX

ST. PETER, ST. JOHN, AND ST. PAUL

X (pp. 7, 8, 9) has it that *St. John seems to see deeper into the mysteries of the faith than the rest* (St. Peter included), and that *for " deep teaching," for " theology," one would have gone to the* Theologos, " *the Divine* " ; and how, in later *Acts,* " *St. Paul fills the canvas* " ; and how he (St. Paul) " *is the authoritative teacher of Asia, Rome, Cyprus* " ; etc.

Now, I think I have shown—under No. VII—

that part of St. John's " theology " is the doctrine of the primacy, still held in A.D. 90–100, and, from Döllinger under No. VIII, that St. Paul's authoritative teaching—that its authority, though direct from our Lord, came also from St. Peter. But more is involved in the matter than this. It seems to me that to get it thoroughly and steadily clear and right is almost equivalent to being a Papist.

Let me quote Cardinal Newman :

It is individuals, and not the Holy See, that have taken the initiative, and given the lead to the Catholic mind, in theological inquiry. Indeed, it is one of the reproaches urged against the Roman Church, that it has originated nothing, and has only served as a sort of *remora* or break in the development of doctrine. And it is an objection which I really embrace as a truth ; for such I conceive to be the main purpose of its extraordinary gift. It is said, and truly, that the Church of Rome possessed no great mind in the whole period of persecution. Afterwards, for a long while, it has not a single doctor to show : St. Leo, its first, is the teacher of one point of doctrine ; St. Gregory, who stands at the very extremity of the first age of the Church, has no place in dogma or philosophy. The great luminary of the western world is, as we know, St. Augustine ; he, no infallible teacher, has formed the intellect of Christian Europe ; indeed, to the African Church generally we must look for the best early exposition of Latin ideas. Moreover, of the African divines, the first in order of time, and not the least influential, is the strong-minded and heterodox Tertullian. Nor is the Eastern intellect, as such, without its share in the formation of the Latin teaching. The free thought of Origen is visible in the writings of the western Doctors, Hilary and Ambrose ; and the independent mind of Jerome has enriched his own vigorous commentaries on Scripture from the stores of the scarcely orthodox Eusebius. Heretical questionings have been transmuted by the living power of the Church into salutary truths. (13)

And this phenomenon is not escaped by simply refusing Roman teaching :

The case is the same as regards Ecumenical Councils. Authority in its most imposing exhibition, grave bishops, laden with the traditions and rivalries of particular nations or places, have been guided in their decisions by the commanding genius of individuals, sometimes young and of inferior rank. Not that uninspired intellect over-ruled the superhuman gift which was committed to the Council, which would be a self-contradic-tory assertion, but that in that process of inquiry and deliberation, which ended in an infallible enunciation, individual reason was paramount. Thus Malchion, a mere presbyter, was the in-strument of the great Council of Antioch in the third century, in meeting and refuting, for the assembled Fathers, the heretical patriarch of that See. Parallel to this instance is the influence, so well known, of the young deacon, St. Athana-sius, with the three hundred and eighteen Fathers at Nicæa. In mediæval times we read of St. Anselm at Bari as the champion of the Council there held, against the Greeks. At Trent, the writings of St. Bonaventura, and, what is more to the point, the address of a priest and theologian, Salmeron, had a critical effect on some of the definitions of dogma. In some of these cases the influence might be partly moral, but in others it was that of a discursive knowledge of ecclesiastical writers, a scientific acquaintance with theology, and a force of thought in the treatment of doctrine. (14)

It seems strange to a Papist to notice how all but

impossible it is to a non-Papist to keep clear in his head—*as against Popery*—the distinction between the essentially *negative* prerogative of inerrancy and the positive gifts and acquirements of grace and genius, or, what amounts pretty much to the same thing, between the so-called *gratia gratis data* and *gratia sanctificans*. I say, " as against Popery," for High Churchmen find no difficulty in the doctrine when applied within their own system. They do not, indeed cannot, mean that the Holy Spirit only guides the assembled bishops of the undivided Church, in this sense, that He sees to their always being the most saintly men and the greatest theological geniuses of their time, and, when these most active and influential representatives of their time are together, adds a still further light to their already predominant insight. In this case they would have to hold with Papists to the negative conception, of their being not necessarily ahead or even abreast of their times, but that even where they are that it is not through this as the necessary and supernatural (?) means that they are guaranteed from error, but by the Holy Spirit keeping their ignorance or passion from producing any positive or final bad result, any actual error, in a final definition. Now, if this holds good, has to suffice, for a Council, why not for a Pope ? And, indeed, not to go to final enactments, is it really necessary to look upon the bishop of each diocese as necessarily the chief luminary and prime instigator of all Church life within it ?   Is it not enough that he should be, necessarily and always, the *flywheel*, and only accidentally and ideally, the *driving-wheel* of the machine ?   And if a bishop in his diocese, why not the Pope in the Church ?

I much preferred talking with Cardinal Newman to any possible talk with Pius IX, just as X would (quite rightly ; so would I) have preferred to consult St. John rather than St. Peter about any deep point in theology.   But I fail to see in either case any shadow of inconsistency with the highest Roman doctrine, unless we specially start a little superstition of our own that the Pope is inerrant even as—not only a private doctor—but as a converser ; or, again, hold (as I always reluctantly suspect High Churchmen half hold) that it is, after all, special and continuous unusual personal holiness and theological learning and insight which are the necessary antecedents and conditions of not only the Church's life (which is true) but also of the final *regulation* of that life (which is not true).

The hearth is not the fire, the vine-stem is not

55

the grape, the soil is not the grain : but without the hearth or the stem or the soil—all three unobtrusive and " dull " conditions—you will have no large yet but warming and undestructive fire, no grapes, no grain. It is part of the very argument for Popery that it is a dish continually producing a pudding that overflows it, a fountain giving out waters that hide the fountain itself. Who thinks of Pope Eugenius or forgets St. Bernard of Clairvaux ? Who remembers the mostly dreary Avignon popes (one of them was a saint) and does not glow at the thought of St. Catherine of Sienna ? Look at the corrupt fifteenth-century popes and that unapproached refinement of ecstatic love, St. Catherine of Genoa. And, further back, how little we care for even the great figure of Innocent III, beside that of the Christ-like Francis of Assisi. And this is, apart from sin, as it should be and as it usually ever will be. The whole Church machinery, popes inclusive, is but a means to the end of the production of saintly souls. And it ought not to be hard to see that it is through union with these often obscure, always human, sometimes positively wicked representatives of a transcendent principle that the largest and deepest Christians have been produced.

X

THE FIRST CENTURY OF THE ROMAN CHURCH

I come now to the first hundred years or so of the history of the Roman See. X says : " *All the time the early heresies were rife, the Roman Pontiff was dumb : not a word from him is recorded to do anything to solve the perplexities of the Faith. And all this time, so we are asked to believe, he had only to open his mouth and the truth would infallibly have been declared, and not only infallibly declared but at once accepted by all true Catholics. But he said nothing. Is this credible ? "*

To this I will make four counter-suggestions.

(i) Is this an argument that can be urged and driven home, I mean by a dogmatic and ecclesiastical Christian ?

The primacy consisting of a doctrine and of an institution, let us see the kind of evidence, and the sort of antiquity all Trinitarians and Episcopalians can urge for their tenets—a doctrine and an institution respectively.

(*a*) The doctrine of the Holy Trinity is the most fundamental of all the Christian doctrines in the eyes of Papists as of all other dogmatic Christians.

57

It is no doubt contained in the New Testament ; it was equally certainly taught by the ante-Nicene Fathers, but often how incompletely, obscurely, confusedly, positively incorrectly ! I do not know of one of the Apologists who is completely satisfactory. I am not, of course, thinking of Synodal decrees or of such writers as St. Athanasius, the deacon. Well, and it takes three centuries, whatever theory you may hold as to Church authority, to get this fundamental doctrine quite completely, clearly, correctly enunciated by all. It is no adequate rejoinder to say " You see, I am right ; only when all the bishops of Christendom unite and define does anything adequate get done " ; for I am not now thinking as to how the fact affects the primacy, but how it affects all who hold that our Lord committed to His Apostles and their successors the deposit of doctrine, the chief article of this deposit being beyond doubt the doctrine of the Holy Trinity. Is it credible, I think one might fairly urge—upon those that attempt to urge the silence and apparent haltingness of Rome at first—that this doctrine of the Holy Trinity should have been in the heads and hearts of the Apostles and all their successors, and, for three hundred years, no fully adequate and steady universal testimony to the correct doctrine should be findable, e.g., in the numerous writings of the Apologists of the second century ? I could easily show you abundant quotations in Petau, Newman, Hefele, Kuhn, and Duchesne, which prove this point clearly as against the Anglican Bishop Bull and the Papist Bishop Bossuet.

(b) The institution of the episcopate dates, according to Anglicans as well as Papists, right back to our Lord, and is one of the Church's fundamental features. Well, and in the *Doctrine of the Twelve Apostles*, a document discovered not twenty years ago, which all admit to be genuine, and which cannot be older than 130—indeed, it may come down to 140 : it is probably Egyptian, but this is uncertain—you *find no trace* of the three orders (of divine institution) of bishop, priest, and deacon ; and instead of them you have three quite distinct orders of apostle, prophet, and teacher, of which evidently the first two have a roving commission, and only the third is localized. Now the New Testament has also unmistakeable indications of these three orders (*Acts* xiii, 1, *ff.* ; *I Corinthians* xii, 28 ; *Ephesians* ii, 20 and iii, 5) and the *Pastor* of Hermas. Again, even Harnack, the great rationalist critic, admits that " there were already

59

episcopi in the Apostolic age, and that not every *presbyter* was an *episcopus*." Still, the broad fact remains that, a full hundred years after our Lord's ascension, we have not simply no evidence for the universal prevalence of episcopacy, but we have irrefragable evidence that in some places (countries), or at least one country, there existed three *other* orders and not one of the divinely instituted orders. I ask an Episcopalian : According to your position —is this credible ?

(ii) The Trinitarian and Episcopalian will have to answer : Our Lord instituted His Church for all time ; all the fundamental institutions and doctrines of the Church existed in the practice and teaching of the Church from the first, but not as universally, explicitly, completely, as in course of time. It is enough for us, if we show you that these institutions and doctrines were intended by our Lord, if we show you traces of them in the Apostolic and Primitive Church, and if in course of time they become universally perceptible. Yes, they will have to say that, both as to the Holy Trinity up to 320, and as to episcopacy up to about a hundred years earlier.

Now what is sauce for the Roman goose is

sauce for the Anglican gander. We require no different *kind* of principle and test for the primacy than we both require for the Trinity and episcopacy; I purposely say different *kind* and not *degree*, and yet I hardly think there is an appreciable difference of *degree* either.

The fact is that we cannot get on without development : all three doctrines and institutions can be shown to have existed from the first, and if there is more evidence for the doctrine of the Holy Trinity, there are also more passages demanding a patient handling.

(iii) X writes as though the Pope had but to open his mouth, and he would speak infallibly and be believed by all to be infallible, during that first century, according to Roman principles. I think this is not so, in three respects :

(*a*) The preamble of the very Vatican definition declares how it has ever been the custom and duty of the Roman pontiffs, before any definition, to consult the bishops and churches, to call synods, etc. : it would be a *grave sin* on the part of any Pope to speak, without such previous steps, even if the case were grave and urgent. Now we know nothing as to what was or was not feasible as to

61

such consultations, etc., during those very obscure hundred years or so.

(*b*) We cannot know what, and whether any, pronouncement would have been prudent under the circumstances.

(*c*) The Roman bishops had no doubt from the first a consciousness of their prerogative, but it does not at all follow that the consciousness of this same prerogative was as universal, as explicit, and as constant throughout the Church as it is now. Indeed, the Church's organization and her consciousness both grew and have grown : this was the early, embryo stage. X requires such a stage just as really as we.

(iv) It is not the case that the Roman bishops did nothing for the Faith during the first hundred years ; if you will look in Harnack's *Dogmenge-schichte*, you will find :

(1) Of the Roman community we know—and in this case alone do we possess perfect certainty —that it possessed a distinctly formulated baptismal creed which, already about 180, it put forward as the Apostolic rule by which everything must be judged. It was recognized accordingly that the Roman Church was able to

distinguish with peculiar accuracy true from false doctrine. Already Ignatius says of the Roman Christians, and only of them, that they are "strained clear" [Lightfoot] from every foreign colour. ["The colour refers to the colouring matter which pollutes the water." Lightfoot (*Ep. ad Rom. Inscr.*).]

(2) The existence of the Canon of the New Testament with Apostolic and Catholic sanctions and exclusive recognition can first be proved for the Roman Church and only later for the other communities.

(3) It is at Rome that we can first prove the existence of a regular list of bishops going back to the Apostles. (Irenæus.)

And he adds some further points. (15)

XI

THE APOSTOLIC FATHERS AND IRENÆUS

Before proceeding to St. Victor's case, I want to put together certain expressions and actions and concessions concerning the Apostolic Fathers—the spiritual grandsons of our Lord. Indeed, these testimonies might well have appeared even before those last given and in continuation of the significant quotation from one of the Apostolic Fathers, St.

Ignatius, here given as taken by Harnack and Lightfoot.

(i) There is that other expression of Ignatius, addressed to the Roman Church, as only to her—that double recurrence of the verb *presides*—as to which Harnack, impartial above all suspicions, says :

In the address which introduces Ignatius's *Epistle to the Romans* the term *preside* is twice used of the Roman community : " which has the presidency in the capital of the Roman empire " [I am giving the Greek as literally as I can : it either means this, or, as Lightfoot takes it, " in the country of the Romans," limiting the range of presidence ; the first translation, a very possible one, makes the presidence universal] ; " the presidency in love," whether the community of love [i.e. Christendom] be intended, or as taking the leading part in works of charity. This same term *preside* is used by Ignatius (*Magnes*. VI) to denote the dignity of the bishop or the presbyters in relation to the rest of the community. Moreover, Bishop Abercius of Hierapolis in Asia Minor speaks of the Roman community in his epitaph as " the Queen." (16)

64

(ii) St. Clement of Rome's *Epistle* (the first :
for the so-called second is neither by Clement nor
an Epistle !) written certainly between A.D. 93–97.

As to the tone and drift of the letter, let me
quote Abbé Duchesne with his extract from
Renan (Duchesne is defending his book *Origines
du Culte Chrétien* against a Huguenot savant,
M. Sabatier) :

As regards St. Clement I am censured for
saying that he writes like a pope, and even for
saying that he is the author of the letter tra-
ditionally attributed to him. One need not,
however, be completely blinded by Catholic
prejudices to speak as I have. " Not only was
Clement of Rome a historical character, he was
a man of the first rank, a true ruler of the Church,
a bishop, before the episcopate was fully constituted, I might even say a pope, if in this connection the word were not too great an anachro-
nism." Who wrote those words ? A protonotary
apostolic ? No, M. Renan (*Évangiles*, p. 312).
His remark on the term *pope* is fully justified in
the sense he understands the word, namely a
mediæval pope of the type of Gregory VII or
Innocent IV. But, once again, a fact is not

F

altered by a question of terminology, and in this instance the fact is simply the authority of the Roman Church, in whatever stage of development its internal organization may be or the organs by which its action on Christendom is manifested. The same M. Renan also says of Clement's *Epistle* : " Few writings are so well authenticated." (17)

(iii) St. Polycarp, Bishop of Smyrna, was the immediate disciple of St. John the Evangelist. Bishop Lightfoot gives his dates thus :

Polycarp was born more than 30 years before the close of the first century, and he survived to the latter half of the second. The date of his birth may be fixed with some degree of certainty as A.D. 69 or 70. At all events it cannot have been later than this. His martyrdom is now ascertained to have taken place A.D. 155 or 156. (18)

And we not only know for certain that he was the immediate disciple of St. John, but we also know from St. Irenæus, Polycarp's immediate disciple (given in Eusebius, *H.E.*, v, 20 ; you can read the English translation of it in Lightfoot *loc. cit.* p. 96), how vivid and detailed was his—

Polycarp's—remembrance and rehearsal of his great master's spirit, words, and even tricks of manner.

Now this very Polycarp, in his extreme old age, goes to Rome. Let me cite Harnack :

The eminent bishop Polycarp did not shrink from the toil of a long journey to secure communion with the Roman Church which was in jeopardy. For other important journeys to Rome of Christians and of bishops in the second and third centuries see Caspari, *Quellen zur Geschichte des Taufsymbols*, vol. III. In particular we would call attention to the journey of Bishop Abercius of Hierapolis about 200 or even earlier which is incontestably historical. It was not Anicetus who came to Polycarp, but Polycarp to him. (19)

(iv) St. Irenæus, Bishop of Lyons, was the direct disciple of Polycarp. And not only so, but we know from his (Irenæus's) letter, given by Eusebius, that his memory as to the teachings of his master Polycarp was as vivid as Polycarp's memory was with regard to the teachings of St. John.

Now, Bishop Lightfoot tells us that Irenæus published the third book of his great work *Against the Heresies* " before A.D. 190 at all events, and possibly some years earlier." (20)

Well, in that third book (III, iii, 2) occurs the well-known passage about the Roman Church :

With this Church, on account of her supremacy [" greater principality," some would translate. I find that Professor Thiersch is sure that " *supremacy* " and nothing else stood in the lost Greek original : see Steiner, I, p. 429b—but in any case the sense of the words is clear] it is necessary that every church, that is the faithful everywhere, should be in communion, in which Church has ever been preserved by the faithful everywhere that tradition which is from the Apostles.

(You can see in Lightfoot's *Ignatius*, II, i, p. 191a, that he also takes " the greater principality " to mean nothing less than the idea of the *cathedra Petri*—precedence over the churches of Christendom.)

You will notice that Irenæus's passage was written a good twenty-five years after his master Polycarp's journey to Rome. It would then never do to not only take " *convenire* " as " resort to " instead of " agree with " or " be in communion with " (indeed either of the three translations will

68

do) but to understand the " *undique* " of the Latin translation (all we have got) of the parts about Rome or Italy and Gaul ; " *undique* " *must* include at least Asia Minor : and if so, " everywhere "—the anyhow *prima facie* correct translation of the word—will alone do.

And, as you know, Irenæus gives a list of the Roman bishops right up to SS. Peter and Paul, and whether this list is in every respect accurate or not, one thing is as plain as day : Irenæus has already the doctrine of the Apostolic Succession fully developed in his head.

(v) Well, now, please pause again a moment and reckon up what these numbers (iii) and (iv), added up with what we have had about the last chapter of the Fourth Gospel, come to.

We have, A.D. 90–100, St. John finishing up with the great scene of the reinstitution of Peter in the primacy—twenty-five years and more after St. Peter's death.

We have, A.D. about 150, that very St. John's own devoted disciple, St. Polycarp, coming all the way from Smyrna to Rome, to the obscure Anicetus.

We have A.D. about 180 that very St. Polycarp's

devoted disciple telling us of SS. Peter (and Paul) and their successors and of the Roman Church being the pattern for the faith of all the churches —that they have all to be in communion with or agree with her.

Surely these three spiritual generations are handing down one common doctrine, and Polycarp did and Irenæus taught only what St. John meant.

XII

BISHOP VICTOR AND THE ASIATICS

As to Bishop Victor and the Asiatics, I will quote Duchesne (still against Sabatier) :

In the matter of the Asiatics I am charged with having said " the opposite of the truth." Now the following is what we know of the relations between the churches of Asia and the Church of Rome in the second century, at least so far as the question before us is concerned.

1. St. Polycarp, Bishop of Smyrna and the disciple of St. John, visited Rome when over eighty years old to discuss with Pope Anicetus several questions, particularly that of Easter.

2. Their conversations having left several points of divergence, the Bishop of Rome, Victor, some forty years later, invited the churches

of the different parts of the Empire, particularly those of Asia, to summon councils to examine the question. Everywhere his wish was carried out, in Asia as elsewhere.

3. With the single exception of the council in Asia, agreement with the Roman Church was universally expressed. The Asiatics maintained their opinion in a letter which one of their number, Polycrates, Bishop of Ephesus, drew up in very strong terms.

4. Victor threatened to excommunicate them, a step for which some of his colleagues blamed him, particularly St. Irenæus.

5. The Asiatics yielded and adopted the Roman custom.

(That the Asiatics yielded at this time is proved by the following facts :

1. At the opening of the fourth century their custom was in conformity with the Roman, and we cannot point to any event during the century preceding which explains the change. *Cf.* my monograph, *La Question de la Pâque au Concile de Nicée*, esp. pp. 14, 21–26.

2. The writers on heresies at the beginning of the third century (the *Philosophumena*, Pseudo-Tertullian) describe the Quartodecimans as a

small sect, not an important group such as the churches of Asia.)

What does this history prove ? That the Asiatics refused for a time to conform on a ritual question to the Roman custom but abandoned their opposition when the question of communion was raised. I cannot see that there is anything to support M. Sabatier's thesis that " the authority of the bishops of Rome as the result of a slow development and long conflicts was raised above that of their colleagues, who were originally their equals." " Their equals " —that is very easy to say. In fact history shows us St. Polycarp visiting Rome in spite of his age and high personal standing to confer with Bishop Anicetus. It never shows us a pope visiting Smyrna or Ephesus to confer with the bishops of these churches. It informs us that the bishops of Asia, though vehemently opposed to the Roman custom, assembled a council at the demand of the Pope ; it does not inform us that any bishop of Ephesus requested the Pope to investigate in council a question of Church discipline. It informs us that the authority of the Church of Rome, even when exercised tactlessly—we will grant that point, though it is

72

by no means indisputable—overcame in Asia an opposition which appealed to the most venerable traditions ; it does not inform us that the Asiatics compelled the Romans to change a single one of their customs. I fail to understand by what method of interpretation a historian can assert the equality of powers which behaved so differently. (21)

And Harnack says very well of Victor's action and its presuppositions :

How could Victor have ventured on an edict of this kind . . . unless it was already acknowledged beyond question that when questions of faith were to be settled the Roman Church possessed the chief voice in determining the conditions of the κοινὴ ἕνωσις (the communion of the Universal Church) ? How could Victor have addressed so unprecedented a demand to independent communities, if he as Bishop of Rome was not recognized as in a unique sense the guardian of the κοινὴ ἕνωσις ? (Even Irenæus does not appear to blame Victor's procedure as such, but only under the particular circumstances.) (22)

Harnack in the second line of the above quotation has " he was not sufficiently powerful to secure

73

universal obedience " (23), but I think Duchesne has fully proved that either all, or at least the overwhelming bulk, of the Asiatics submitted, and submitted soon.

XIII

THE ROMAN CHURCH IN THE FIRST THREE CENTURIES

I am surprised to find X saying (pp. 13, 14) :

" *The Church is torn asunder by the Arian heresy. . . . The Bishop of Rome is dumb.*" This reads to me as if he meant to say that not till Nicæa was anything done to officially safeguard the doctrine of the Holy Trinity, by popes, and even at the Council not by popes.

But this is simply not the fact. Let me again quote Duchesne (he is meeting the objection raised from the eccentric teaching of the Apologists of the second century, also Origen, St. Denys of Alexandria, and others as to the Holy Trinity). He says :

The true, the hierarchical tradition, that of the infallible and living *magisterium*, pursued its course on the Trinitarian question regardless of the private views of these writers. These private opinions, grafted by the individual writer in one fashion or another on the official teaching, in no way involve the responsibility of the latter.

74

It will be replied that my distinction between the infallible *magisterium* of the Church and private individuals indeed solves many difficulties, but that it is not easy to point to any effective intervention of the *magisterium* during the first centuries. . . .

To that I reply that there is at least one instance, certain, clear, and universally admitted, namely the letter of Pope St. Dionysius to his namesake Dionysius, Bishop of Alexandria.

Pope Callistus said to certain teachers " You are ditheists," without however excommunicating them for their doctrine. For this we have the wholly disinterested testimony of one of the censured, the author of the *Philosophumena*. The censure, in conjunction with the absence of any formal condemnation, proves that there was no question of a real ditheism, which would have been immediately condemned, but of a teaching which, contrary to the intention of its propounders, endangered the doctrine of the Divine Unity. By similar arguments M. de Rossi reached the same conclusion before me.

The third instance is far less clear. Pope Fabian felt doubts as to the doctrines of Origen, and that doctor was obliged to defend his orthodoxy before him. We do not know what exactly was the point at issue. But it is certain that ever since the fourth century writers of the highest authority continued to stigmatize as erroneous his doctrine on the Trinity. (24)

Now, X was free to overlook the last two, or at least the middle instance. But the first ought certainly to have been given.

Of it the very accurate Fr. X. Kraus says :

On the complaint of certain Egyptian brethren the Roman Bishop Dionysius assembled in 262 a synod at Rome in which, as also in a personal letter, he condemned the form of expression employed by Bishop Dionysius of Alexandria (at a synod held in Alexandria in 261) to describe the relationship of the Son to God the Father, and defended the unity of essence as alone in harmony with the Faith. As the result of this instruction the Bishop of Alexandria retracted his explanation and adopted the Pope's. (25)

XIV

THE FIRST THREE GENERAL COUNCILS

As to the first three General Councils (X, pp. 14, 15).

(i) Nicæa. " *When a Council is called, the Bishop*

of Rome has no part in calling it, and practically no part in its work ; and the great Nicene definition of the Truth takes place without Rome at all."

I notice here, just as in the case of the Council of Jerusalem (p. 5), what seems to me an excessive pressing of negatives. I mean that Papists as well as Anglicans hold Councils to be infallible—Councils of bishops in union with Rome and the decrees approved by Rome. They are *one* of the modes in which the Church expresses her voice. And that God should at one time cause His Church to speak through one means, at another through another, seems nothing so very wonderful. I have just shown that sixty-three years before Nicæa the Pope *did* speak, and with the fullest effect, to one so high up as the Bishop of Alexandria.

Another point altogether, of course, would be to urge that the Pope was not represented at the Council, or that his legates did not preside. The latter has been worked at by Protestants for the last three hundred years and more, with the steadiest good will (!) against Rome. But the inner proceedings of the Council are so obscure that we can but go by probabilities, and it has to be a *very* bold Protestant indeed to doubt that these are all in favour of the legates having presided. There is

77

simply no case of an Œcumenical Council, even of the "undivided " Church, in which Rome was not merely unrepresented, but in which her substitute or legates did not preside (Hefele, i, 29–44).

(ii) Constantinople (I).

Here I deny both X's contentions.

(*a*) As to Rome not having presided, Hefele says excellently :

We admit without question that at the second General Council neither the Pope (Damasus) nor his legate presided, for admittedly this Council was not intended to be œcumenical but simply to be a general council of the Eastern Church. (26)

But you can find it all in full detail in Hefele's vol. II, which you have got.

(*b*) As to St. Meletius, if you will look up in Ryder (p. 59 it is of my edition of *Catholic Controversy*), or, better still because longer, in Hefele, vol. II, you will see that this second point also is not worthy of the higher controversialists : it is good enough for Littledale, no doubt.

(iii) As to Ephesus. It is surely not necessary for the Pope to preside over a General Council in person. I suppose Trent was fully papal ? And yet it was presided over simply by legates. Why is the Pope's authority uncertain because of his investing St. Cyril with his (the Pope's) authority in addition to Cyril's own ? If you will, in this case also, look it all up in Hefele : vol. II (or possibly III) and look there (or in Ryder, p. 15) at what Philip, the legate, says to the Council (I have never heard of objections being taken to it) —you will see that Ephesus also ought to have been left out of X's list.

(iv) But Chalcedon, A.D. 451—look that up with care : it is the fourth Œcumenical Council, or rather the third, counting those that were œcumenical from the very opening (you will find it in Hefele's volumes, or, the special point, in Ryder, p. 16)—and Pope Agatho (680) in his letter read at the sixth General Council (Ryder, p. 19) : was the Holy Spirit not with these Councils, too ? It is really quite bad enough to get to the thousand years' suspension of inerrant Church teaching by A.D. 800 and some odd years, without refusing to let Councils of the " undivided " Church speak up for the primacy just now and then.

XV

SHORT SUMMING UP

I dare not go on. The summing up would be : that there is no serious *a priori* reason against the primacy, consistently with a visible-Church position ; that the primacy is undeniable in the Gospels and requires to be, somehow or other, maintained through *Acts* and Epistles ; and that Church history shows us that it was as truly there from the first, but as truly grew and had to face as real difficulties as the other doctrines and institutions. And only through it do you get unsuspended Church authority and full docility and life.

Yours affectionately,

FR. VON HÜGEL.

POST SCRIPTA

THE foregoing *Notes*, written under pressure, are particularly " scamped " towards the end. Some important additions and expansions have occurred to me since : I will put these down as briefly as I can.

I

Addition to IV, *about reasonableness of Papist's acceptance of Vatican definitions.*

Is it possible that some such notion haunts X's mind as that which Mr. Gladstone brought forward, in hot anger, against Rome in his *Expostulation* of 1873 ? He there was mighty sarcastic about how it had been only the decrees of the very Vatican Council which had proclaimed the Pope's inerrancy which were worded " Pius, Bishop, with the approval of the Sacred Council " ; whereas, even down to the very last previous one—the Council of Trent—it had always been " The Sacred Council of —, with the approval of —,

Bishop." So that you had here a delightful cart-before-the-horse affair : the infallible Pope declared infallible on the assumption of his own infallibility. Alas, alas, for the kind intention of Mr. Gladstone ! There is nothing whatever at the back of all this cheap thunder. The matter stands thus. From time immemorial—I cannot give you just now the precise date, but I think it goes back to the ninth General Council (first of the " divided " Church), held in the Lateran in 1123, the first over which a pope presided in person—the invariable rule has been : when an Œcumenical Council is presided over by the Pope in person, the decrees run " Bishop, with the approval of the Sacred Council " ; when the Council is presided over by papal legates only, then the decrees run " The Sacred Council, with the approval of —, Bishop." It just so happened that the Council immediately previous to the Vatican Council had been presided over only by papal legates, and that the Vatican one was presided over by the Pope in person ; hence a difference in the terminology which is to be observed throughout the last twelve of the twenty General Councils : during the first eight no presidence of a pope in person took place at all. You will then see the whole thing is nothing but an instance of men's readiness to speak before they really know—in the matter of the Church.

II

Addition to VI, VII, *on the Gospels : critics' admissions and conclusions therefrom.*

Between the first and second of the texts discussed, I ought to have put *Luke* v, 1–11.

Now, all the Fathers from St. Augustine downwards, and even further back, agree in looking upon this passage as allegorical. Most of them hold it to be strictly historical as well, and distinct from the vocation of *Mark* i, 16–20, *Matthew* iv, 18–22 ; a minority hold it to be an allegorical mosaic worked up from various historical occurrences of our Lord's life and an expansion of *Mark* i and *Matthew* iv. Almost all modern Catholic as well as Protestant commentators take this latter view, and I think they are right. But pray notice that the cogency of what follows is quite unaffected by the question as to the historicity of the section : admit it to be allegorical, and my point is gained.

Holtzmann, who [here] identifies *Mark, Matthew*, and *Luke*—after discussing *Mark* and *Matthew*—come to *Luke* and says :

Luke's account retain the common text only

at the beginning (verse 2, the fishermen busied with their nets on the lake, as in *Mark* i, 17, 20) and the end (verse 10, " fishers of men," and 11, " forsaking . . . they followed Him "). The remainder is painted over with allegorical features.

Instead of the loneliness of the original account, on this occasion also there is a gathering of the multitude by the lake as in *Mark* xi, 13 ; instead of the fishing of one, and the net-repairing of the others, we have here first (verse 2) a common washing of nets (after the end of their work, verse 5), then (verse 7) a common fishing. Of the two boats (verse 2) one belongs (verse 3) to Simon. The unspecified owners of the other must, as is shown by verses 7 and 10, be the sons of Zebedee.

(1) Peter must at first *put out* a little from the shore into the lake, then (verse 4) must do the same again, but now no longer only *a little* so that it is possible to preach to the people of Israel standing on the bank, but *into the deep*, where the lake is deep and the fish, which represent the Gentiles, can be caught. Thus the history of the Apostles' vocation is transformed into an allegory of their world mission, and the

conversion of the Gentiles in particular is represented as a direct command of Jesus.

(2) Moreover, the fact that in this Lucan remoulding of the account the preaching of the *word of God* precedes the taking of the fish points to its symbolic content.

(3) As Jesus here must first show Peter the place where he can fish successfully, so in the corresponding story (*Acts* xi, 15) God directs him on the same way.

(4) Peter's original dislike of the mission to the Gentiles as testified by *Acts* x, 13, despite the slight success which attended the primary mission of the Apostles to the Jews, corresponds here with the saying in verse 5.

(5) Usually the night proves the favourable time for successful fishing. Now, however, among the Gentiles the Christian cause prospers for the first time (verse 6). The net however breaks. This is an allusion, occasioned by the incident (*Mark* i, 19 ; *Matthew* iv, 21), to the rent with which the question of the Gentiles and the Law threatened the Church. So at any rate this feature of the narrative was understood by the later writer, who after the danger had been removed wrote (*John* xxi, 11) " *it did not*

break." *Cf.* also *Matthew* xiii, 47 (the Church a net).

(6) The partners whom Peter (verse 7) must first draw after him into the new path are, according to verse 10, the sons of Zebedee, and generally the rest of the original Apostles and the representatives of the primitive community. *Cf.* their scruples as to Peter's action (*Acts* x, 45 ; xi, 2).

(7) Peter himself, amazed at his success, trembles in Jesus's presence. His awe (verse 9) in the presence of the divine is shared (verse 10) by the sons of Zebedee. This represents the original fear and later amazement of the Pillars (*Galatians* xi, 9) when faced by the effects of God's work among the Gentiles.

(8) The simple saying (*Mark* i, 19), the historical foundation of the entire narrative, which is here transformed into sensible imagery and ingenious allegory, is now addressed to Peter alone. (27)

Now let me underline some of these points.

Here is St. Luke writing twenty and more years after the occurrences at Jerusalem and Antioch, indeed, ten years or so after St. Peter's and St. Paul's deaths, who is so utterly unaware of the High Anglican " conclusive " proofs as to

the non-existence or at least non-persistence of the
primacy that, in a passage peculiar to himself, and
one which has at all times been held to be either
historical *and* allegorical or (almost purely) allegorical, he gives us a prophetic picture of St. Peter's
action in which St. Peter stands first from first
to last.

For notice : our Lord mounts into *Peter's* boat,
not that of the Beloved Disciple ; our Lord orders
Peter, and not Andrew (yet Andrew had been the
first called in the preliminary vocation given in
John i, 35–42), first to push off to a short distance
and then far out ; He preaches to the people from
Peter's boat ; it is *Peter* that He orders to throw
out the nets and catch the fish ; it is *he* who catches
all that quantity of fish ; it is *he* who called the
Beloved Disciple and his other partners to his aid :
they are simply his seconds and subordinates ; it
is *Peter* who is first seized with holy fear ; it is to
Peter (and, in St. Luke, to *Peter alone*) that our
Lord says he shall henceforth catch men. [See
additional note, page 96.]

I ought also to have drawn your attention to
Mark i, 29–31 ; ii, 1 ; iii, 20 ; ix, 33.

Of the first passage Holtzmann says :

" Straightway " (verse 29).   Immediately on

leaving the synagogue Jesus enters Simon's
house, which will soon become His home also
(in accordance with His own instructions, *Mark*
iv, 10 ; *Luke* ix, 4), and the starting point of
His work in Capernaum. (28)

There he gives the further references I have just
given.

As to this first passage, or rather verse 45 of
chapter i, Meyer-Weiss says, " No doubt Simon's
house is intended " ; as to the second (*Mark* ii, 1),
" probably Simon's house." (29)

Now this, of course, means that, just as St. Luke
has shown us that the Church both of Jew and
Gentile is Peter's, and that it is in Peter's Church
that our Lord lives on and on—so that here we
learn, as a bit of certain history, that our Lord
began His preaching from Peter's house and made
that His first headquarter. I think we will do well
to still look for Him where His Apostles and their
disciples were wont to seek and find Him.

III

Correction in VIII, *as to Acts and Epistles* (*towards
end*).

In illustration of the admitted fallibility of the
Popes *qua governors*, I took the cases of the excom-

munications of Elizabeth and Victor Emmanuel as not beyond the reach of mistake according to even the very strictest Roman doctrine. This is all right ; but I ought to have said St. Pius V instead of Sixtus V in the first case. The change only strengthens my point.

IV

Additions to X, *as to the first hundred years of the Roman Church.*

(i) Here I ought to have pointed out, as a most obvious reason for such silence as can be fairly charged against the Roman Church of this time, the fact that not only was this the period, above all others, of the growth and organization of even the most elementary of the offices and functions of the Church, in *Rome as much as elsewhere* ; but also that it was a period of persecution and of living from hand to mouth, in *Rome more than elsewhere.* It is, then, something like asking miners who have attained to Trades Congresses, and who from the first held and discussed among themselves, more or less informally, similar views within the mines and when struggling for their daily livelihood, why, if they held these views from the first, they cannot point to Trades Union Congresses and

official decisions from the first. You can find all
we know about the martyr popes in Duchesne's
great edition of the *Liber Pontificalis* I, pp. lxxxix–
ci ; and you can there see how, exaggerated as the
ancient belief is that *all* the popes up to St. Sylvester
were martyrs, yet the number of probable and
even certain martyrs among them, especially during
these hundred years, is great.

(ii) I ought also, in giving from Harnack what
the Roman Church of this and the next ante-Nicene
period can be shown to *have* done, to have not
broken off at his No. 3 of the seven things he gives,
but to have quoted also the last four. Here they
are :

(4) The idea of the apostolic succession of
bishops was first employed by the bishops of
Rome, and in connection with it the political
conception of the Church first distinctly formulated by them. The utterances and corresponding practical measures of Callistus (Hippolytus)
and Stephen are the earliest of their kind. The
definite conviction with which they substituted
the political clerical concept of the Church for
the ideal, or fused it with the latter, the firmness
with which they proclaimed the sovereign power
of the episcopate, was not exceeded in the third

century even by Cyprian. (Note : the fact that the idea of the apostolic succession of bishops was first utilized, if it did not arise, at Rome, is the more remarkable since it was by no means in Rome but rather in the East that the monarchical episcopate first took shape—*cf.* the *Shepherd* of Hermas and Ignatius's *Epistle to the Romans*, with the other epistles of Ignatius. The constitutional development in Rome must therefore have been rapid during the period between Hyginus and Victor.)

(5) It is to a Roman bishop that the Eastern churches attribute the composition of the most important part (the eighth book) of the *Apostolic Constitutions* for the organization of the Church, and perhaps not without warrant. (Note : we must also remember the important part ascribed by the tradition both of the Eastern and Western churches to the oldest Roman bishop, Clement, as confidant and secretary of the Apostles.)

(6) The excessive claims of the Roman bishop Callistus were rejected by the three leading theologians of the period, Tertullian, Hippolytus, and Origen. Their attitude proves that the progress in the work of giving the Church a political character, which Callistus's measures

denoted, was at the time an unheard-of innovation. Nevertheless, his action *immediately* exercised an extremely important influence on the attitude of other churches. It is certain that in the following decade they had all taken the same step forward.

(7) In Rome first arose the institution of the inferior clergy (doorkeeper, reader, acolyte, exorcist), and with it the distinction between the *clerici majores* (bishop, priest, deacon) and the *clerici minores*. But it is certain that this institution, so pregnant with consequences, gradually spread throughout the Church. (Note : the canons of Nicæa presuppose the distinction between the higher and lower clergy as existing throughout the Church.) (30)

A word or two about these seven points of Harnack's.

You will notice that they are all (Apostles' Creed ; New Testament canon ; episcopal lists ; apostolic succession ; *Apostolic Constitutions* ; growth of these three latter ideas throughout the Church ; major and minor orders) as much part and parcel of the High Church position as of our own.

And Harnack is quite right in looking upon their

development as slow and fitful, and originally local —just as the " branch " theorists regard the development of the further Papist doctrines and institutions.

And, again, he is quite right in tracing the first full development and articulation of these doctrines, still common to us Papists and the other " branches," to the Roman Church ; so that in a very true sense the Church was *first Roman and then Catholic*.

And just as the " branch " theorists will have it that the Papacy only grew out of the episcopate, and was a mushroom growth upon it, sucking its life-blood from it—so Harnack holds that the episcopate (monarchical), in Rome as elsewhere, grew out of the community, and was a mushroom growth upon *it*. And, certainly, both views are equally false or equally true.

And, finally, Harnack's No. 6 can only be held to be conclusive by such Unitarians (he is practically that, denying all miracles and our Lord's deity) as himself. For Tertullian was a Montanist ; Origen held the most inexact views as to the Holy Trinity (besides that, his appearing before Pope Fabian, he, the celebrated teacher, all the way from the Far East, to answer for his orthodoxy, would tend to show how his opposition to Rome must not be pressed beyond *disciplinary* matters) ; and as to Hippolytus—the authorship of the *Philosophumena* is so little certain that the book has been attributed, beside Hippolytus, to Origen (so Cruice at first), or Caius (so Bishop Lightfoot at one time), or Novatian, or finally Tertullian (so Cruice later on, and above all de Rossi)—in the case of the first and last of these four alternatives we have not " *three* leading " but only *two* " theologians " ; and the doctrine of the author of the book, whoever he may be, as to the Holy Trinity, is again unsatisfactory. It is true he attacks two popes—Zephyrinus violently and Callistus very violently—for both of them stoutly defending the true Trinitarian doctrine : is this alone sufficient to constitute a " leading theologian " ? I hope not, at least, in High Churchmen's eyes.

V

Addition to XIII, *as to the Roman Church during the first three centuries.*

I ought to have made it clear that the dogmatic letter of Pope Denys to Bishop St. Denys of Alexandria, criticizing the latter's Trinitarian doctrine, and which the latter formally submitted to— that this letter and this fact do not simply repose

94

upon learned inference ; or, again, are even directly testified-to facts—bare facts without details : but that we still have the greater part of the letter, given by St. Athanasius in his *Concerning the Decrees of the Synod of Nicæa*, ch. XXVI, and his *Concerning the Decision of Dionysius*, ch. XIII : you can read a *précis* of it in Hefele, Vol. I, pp. 255–257, or in Kraus, p. 75.

VI

Addition to XIV, *as to the first three General Councils.*

The convocation of the Council of Nicæa, and indeed of all the first eight General Councils (of the " undivided " Church), by the Emperor instead of the Pope is not a point which High Churchmen can consistently press. For is such a convocation an ideal one, even according to High Church principles ? Surely it is as little so for them as it is for Papists. With them the *bishops* would be the ideal convokers, with us the *Pope— et voilà toute la différence.*

You would find, too, in Hefele, Vol. I, pp. 8–15, and 44–49, how much there is, in varying degrees and ways, to soften the imperial convocation and approbation of those first eight Councils.

I ought here, on page 87, to have added, as a further note on *Luke* v, 1–11, that it will not do, as an objection to the allegorical character of the narrative, or at least to the Papist use I here would put it to, to urge the " and their nets were breaking " of verse 6, as though this must then mean that the unity of the Church and the primacy within it really came to an end with the Christian-heathen question. It will not do for the following reasons. Meyer–Weiss say very truly :

Verse 6. " Their nets were breaking." The rent actually occurred, but it was only a beginning. The assistance now given prevented further damage. Analogously, verse 7, " that they began to sink." Therefore not to be pressed too far. (31)

And they compare very interestingly :

Luke i, 59, " and they called him after his father's name, Zacharias." They actually uttered this name, but the mother objected (verse 60). The action really begins, but owing to obstacles is not completed (see Schaefer on Euripides, *Phœnissæ*, 81). (32)

I ought also to have quoted Holtzmann on *John* xxi, 1–14 :

Verse 3. As a fisherman by profession and leader of the Apostles Peter speaks. Together with him the others *left* Capernaum to do their fishing by night as in *Luke* v, 5.

Verse 6. " They were not able to draw it," as in *Luke* v, " for the multitude of fishes." As these—see *Mark* i, 17 = *Matthew* iv, 19 = *Luke* v, 10—signify men, this multitude depicts the abundantly blessed fruit of the Gentile mission.

Verse 9. We are not informed how the preparations for the breakfast were made. Did Jesus provide for it by giving the work to Peter ?

According to verse 10 the " fish " of verse 9 proved insufficient. Therefore (verse 11) Peter " went up " into the ship and " drew the net to land." Already Jerome (*In Ezechielem* xlvii, 12) explained their number, which was certainly not accidental, by appealing to writers on natural history, especially to the *Halieutica* (*Art of Fishing*) composed under Marcus Aurelius by Oppianus Cilix, which reckons one hundred and fifty-three species of fish. The number therefore symbolizes the universality of the apostolic mission and represents the " every kind " of the parable of the fishing-net, *Matthew* xiii, 47.

But if in the present case the net, in contrast

to *Luke* v, 6, does not break, we are obliged to see in this an analogue of the coat which could not be divided (xix, 24), and in both pictures a symbolic allusion to the unity of the Church in process of consolidation ; and it is for the same reason that the two boats of *Luke* v, 7 disappear, and instead the entire catch is drawn to land in one net. (33)

Here, again, *Peter* over the whole undivided Church : if there is any change between the writer's view of 70 or 80 (Luke) and that of the writer of A.D. 95 or so (St. John or Johannine writer), it is that the latter, especially if taken with his next passage (xxi, 15–23, already discussed in the *Notes*), is even more emphatically Petrine than the former.

I have done.

Three positions, taking the whole range from dogmatic Atheism up to Popery into account, appear to me to be self-consistent as well as true so far as they are *positive* and as compared with the positions below them.

Agnosticism ; Unitarianism ; Popery : the first as against dogmatic Atheism ; the second as against not only dogmatic Atheism and Agnosti-

cism, but also as against Materialism and even
Pantheism ; the third as against all these and the
various forms of " historical " Christianity as well.
In each case you have the affirmations true and
throughout *identical* ; in each case you have the
negations, when turned against lower negations,
right, when turned against the upper affirmations,
wrong ; in each case the higher stage understands,
or at least can understand, the lower stage ; in
each case the lower stage pooh-poohs and pooh-
bahs the upper stage, counts the flies on the windows
when arguments are brought to bear, and can but
see unreality and superstition in the fuller life.
As Leslie Stephen's tone is towards James Martineau's, so is Martineau's towards Cardinal Newman ;
and so also with the intermediate steps.

In proportion as consistency prevails over preju-
dice, so will " historical " Christians of all schools
have to sink back into Unitarianism (*à la* Hatch
and Harnack) or move on into Popery (*à la* Newman
and Möhler). But the fullest experience of the
soul and the fullest realization of the history of
religion will move them on and not allow them to
sink back.

APPENDIX

REFERENCES FOR PASSAGES QUOTED AND TRANSLATED
IN THE TEXT

(1) de Smedt, " *Organisation des églises au troisième siècle*," *compte rendue du Congrès Scientifique Internationale des Catholiques*, Paris, 1891, section 8, pp. 93, 94.

(2) *Ibid.*, p. 93.

(3) Meyer-Weiss, *Kritisch-exegetischer Kommentar über das Neue Testament*, 7th ed., 1885, I, 2, pp. 331–337.

(4) *Ibid.*, pp. 337, 338.

(5) Holtzmann, *Hand-Commentar zum Neuen Testament*, Freiburg, 1889, I (*Synoptiker*), pp. 193, 194.

(6) Meyer-Weiss, *Kommentar*, I, 2, p. 607.

(7) *Ibid.*, 1886, II, p. 707.

(8) Holtzmann, *Hand-Commentar*, 1891, IV, pp. 203–205.

(9) Harnack, *Dogmengeschichte*, I, 1888, p. 407.

(10) Meyer-Weiss, *Kommentar*, I, 2, p. 145.

(11) Döllinger, *Christenthum und Kirche in der Zeit der Grundlegung*, 1868, pp. 295–298.

(12) *Ibid.*, pp. 63, 64.

(13) Newman, *Apologia*, 1879, p. 265.

(14) *Ibid.*, pp. 265, 266.

(15) Harnack, *Dogmengeschichte*, I, p. 401.

(16) *Ibid.*, p. 404, n. 4.

(17) Duchesne, *Bulletin Critique*, XI, p. 267.

(18) Lightfoot, *Essays on the work entitled " Supernatural Religion,"* Cambridge, 1889, p. 90.

(19) Harnack, *Dogmengeschichte*, I, p. 406, n. 1.

(20) Lightfoot, *Essays on the work entitled " Supernatural Religion,"* p. 259.

(21) Duchesne, *Bulletin Critique*, XI, pp. 265–266.

(22) Harnack, *Dogmengeschichte*, I, p. 408.

(23) *Ibid.*

(24) Duchesne, *Témoins Anté-Nicéens du Dogme de la Trinité*, pp. 44, 45.

(25) Kraus, *Handbuch der . . . Kirchengeschichte*, par. 78.

(26) Hefele, *Conciliengeschichte*, Freiburg, 1873, I, p. 38.

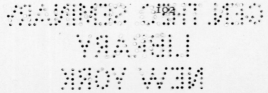

(27) Holtzmann, *Hand-Commentar*, I, pp. 72–74.

(28) *Ibid.*, pp. 76–77.

(29) Meyer-Weiss, *Kommentar*, I, 2, pp. 29, 35.

(30) Harnack, *Dogmengeschichte*, I, p. 402.

(31) Meyer-Weiss, *Kommentar*, I, 2, p. 357.

(32) *Ibid.*, pp. 290–291.

(33) Holtzmann, *Hand-Commentar*, IV, pp. 202–203.

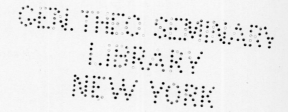